TABLE OF CONTENTS

BIBLIOGRAPHY & ENDNOTES

INTRODUCTION

THE MIGHTY EAGLE...as the storm approaches, lesser fowl head for cover, but the mighty EAGLE spreads his wings and with a great cry mounts on the powerful updrafts, soaring.......

The eagle personified America...soaring, free, strong and powerful. As the eagle soared effortlessly in the midst of the storm so God's people were able to rise on the wings of faith. Faith in God is embedded in American history and culture.

God has showered over two hundred years of blessing upon America. As she acknowledged and obeyed God's plan, she was elevated from infancy to a place of world leadership marked by freedom, unprecedented wealth, and influence.

Then slowly--almost imperceptibly--she began to attribute her blessings not so much to God, but to man.[1] The lines of right and wrong have blurred. We are collectively wallowing in materialism, self-centeredness and pride. "Courts that had once legislated against immorality began to grant freedom to every man to 'do that which was right in his own eyes'(Judges 17:6 and 21:5)."[2] Has our nation's spiritual foundation crumbled? Have our leaders led us astray because they neglected the "spiritual dimension" of leadership? Will an army stand and fight for freedom, democracy, and the American way of life if there is no spiritual backbone?

My research has convinced me more than ever that we need to look back and rediscover the foundational truths behind the success of our nation and the Army. This study examines the "real threat" to our national security - that we are no longer a "nation under God" and are no longer led by those who understand the spiritual dimension of leadership envisioned and demonstrated by our founding fathers.

We talk often of threats to our national security yet seldom discuss what I believe is the greatest threat--the spiritual decay of America. It effects the very fabric of our founding fathers' mosaic. The decay rots away the strengths of our society and the extension of that society -- our armed forces. A central theme of military history is that the first key to understanding any armed force is to understand the society from which it comes. An armed force will be no stronger than the society it serves. A sick society can hardly produce healthy armed forces.[3] Our society is sick.

What was once a nation that was tolerant in the name of civil rights now openly condones and even flaunts perversion, immorality, and a host of attitudes which were once unthinkable. We have turned away from that which made America great--her faith in God coupled with spiritual leadership.

Little by little that faith has turned to "relativism" and "secularism"- not because it was forced upon us, but seemingly because we did not care. Whereas our founding fathers knew the importance of and accepted their role as spiritual leaders and did their best to reflect that in the documents they produced, most leaders today get caught up in the trap of "secular humanism" and neglect their spiritual responsibilities.

What about today's leadership? America's sons and daughters, the strength of our armed forces, will be the big losers unless spiritual leadership becomes an essential quality of our leaders at every level.

In their deliberations on 29 July 1775, Congress recognized the importance of meeting the spiritual needs of the soldiers of the Continental Army by allowing General George Washington to recruit chaplains.[4] General Washington said that faith in God undergirded the Continental Army during the anguish of Valley Forge and "sustained the Revolutionary Army when all else was gone".[5] We would probably be shocked today if Congress openly supported a "spiritual need" through legislation.

What then, is our spiritual responsibility to those we lead? National leaders cannot turn over their responsibilities of spiritual leadership to the "church" any more than military leaders cannot merely turn over the mantle of spiritual leadership to their chaplains. The strength of our nation and the effectiveness of our fighting forces depends on leaders that are spiritually responsible.

3

A SPIRITUAL FOUNDATION

Acting on prior instructions from the government at Williamsburg, on 7 June 1776, Delegate Richard Henry Lee of Virginia introduced a resolution into Congress calling for a declaration of independence. The Congress elected five men to prepare a document claiming nationhood and independence under international law. The five were John Adams, Benjamin Franklin, Roger Sherman, Robert Livingston, and Thomas Jefferson. After discussing what form the declaration would take, the committee appointed Jefferson to write the first draft. Congress approved the final draft and voted independence on July 2, 1776.

The Declaration bore intense resolve and reflected the soul and mind of America. It was written with an understanding that man's law cannot be arbitrary, without insulting the laws of nature and of nature's God. Truth can be known, sometimes so clearly as to be self-evident. God created men, and created them equal, endowing them with inalienable rights- rights that they could not give away and that no one could take from them.

Because God made men and gave them their rights, men create governments under God's law to protect those rights.[6]

America's founding fathers understood very well the principle that faith and freedom go together, and that one cannot survive long without the other. Daniel Webster, the great statesman and orator of the early days of the Republic, in a speech delivered on December 22, 1820, at Plymouth, Massachusetts said,

Finally, let us not forget the religious character of our origin. Our fathers were brought hither by their high veneration for the

4

Christian religion. They journeyed by its light and labored in its hope. They sought to incorporate its principles with the elements of their society and to diffuse its influence through all their institutions, civil, political, or literary. Let us cherish these sentiments, and extend this influence still more widely, in the full conviction that that is the happiest society which partakes in the highest degree of the mild and peaceful spirit of Christianity.[7]

The signers of the Declaration of Independence stated,

We therefore, the Representatives of the United States of America, in General Congress assembled, appealing to the Supreme Judge of the world for the rectitude of our intentions...solemnly publish and declare that these united colonies are, and of right ought to be, free and independent states...And for the support of this Declaration, with a firm reliance on the protection of Divine Providence, we mutually pledge to each other our lives, our fortunes and our sacred honor.[8]

"Supreme Judge of the world," "the protection of Divine Providence," and "sacred honor" were not empty phrases in the minds of the signers. Jefferson and the U.S. Congress were very much concerned that their cause was right with God.

The Declaration is also filled with John Locke's language, as well as his political ideas. His ideas are biblically based, being a devout Christian himself.[9] The Declaration has been called a revolutionary document. But its power came from its affirmation of truth long established.

A key idea in the Declaration of Independence is that of "self-evident truths," truths so clear and obvious to the ordinary person that they require no proof. Ironically, the term "self-evident" is the one that most clearly shows the impact of Christianity on the Declaration.[10]

Thomas Jefferson believed it was sufficient to assert certain transcendent truths as self-evident. To him God's existence was manifest in creation. Jefferson was not here talking about the God of Islam, faith in whom laid the foundation for a different kind of social order altogether. He meant the God of the New Testament. Whether Jefferson was himself a Christian is in dispute, but he understood the society in which he lived and who his audience was.[11] Jefferson was addressing Christians. "Therefore," warns the Apostle Paul in his letter to the Romans, "let every person be in subjection to the governing authorities. For there is no authority except from God..." (Romans 13:1).

The writings of Paul in Romans 1 and 2 are the Biblical source for the Christian belief about self-evident truth. Paul uses two Greek phrases that correspond to the concept of being self-evident. In Romans 1:19 the words "phaneros en autois" mean "evident in themselves" and in Romans 1:20 the words "tois poiemasin nooumena kathoratai" mean "by means of things that are made are understood, being clearly seen".[12]

Paul uses both phrases in the context of what men know naturally by natural revelation, apart from the special revelation of Scripture. The apostle makes it clear that this is a general revelation through nature and through man's conscience. It is a revelation only of the first principles of truth and morality. This revelation comes upon men from God despite man's darkness and sinfulness. Its knowledge does not originate with man, but is a gracious endowment from man's Maker. All men know it naturally, both through conscience and through observing the natural order.[13]

The Declaration of Independence proclaims its rights theory

with the words: "We hold these truths to be self-evident: that all men are created equal; that they are endowed, by their Creator, with certain inalienable rights; that among these are life, liberty, and the pursuit of happiness." These were rights ordained by God in the constitution of the universe. Whether or not the British acknowledged them was irrelevant because these rights were "self-evident" - clear and certain.[14]

Twentieth-century society has lost its foundation for an understanding of "rights". Most see rights as a matter of politics where the government can create and take them away. There is a great deal of talk about "human rights" and "civil rights" but the concept of "unalienable rights" is all but lost. This situation signals a crisis in modern political thought and threatens Western freedoms, since the concept of rights is "theory dependent". [15]

America was founded on "inalienable rights"- those that man may not unconditionally sell, trade, barter, or transfer without denying the image of God in himself.[16] "Inalienable" is another word for eternal, not subject to change under any circumstance. It implies that there are moral absolutes. Today, the rights theory of the founding fathers is routinely traced to secular tradition. Why should Americans care that the Biblical roots of our culture have been exchanged for a wholesale commitment to the prevailing secular philosophy? A major difference is that secular philosophy is based on notions of power, whereas Biblical politics is based on concepts of authority. In the secular view, nothing is ever impermissible because no lines are drawn that cannot be crossed.

7

In secular reasoning, whoever wields power can determine the content of laws, the extent, and even the existence of other people's freedoms. Biblical philosophy, on the other hand, admits to predetermined lines of authority which the civil government is not permitted to cross. Personal rights and freedoms are God-given and inalienable; they do not exist merely for civil convenience or at the discretion of those who hold civil power. Our founding fathers clearly meant for all to maintain these God-given rights and freedoms unconditionally -- not subject to conditional "civil liberties," liberties granted by the government at its own convenience.

The American Revolution is not over. The ideals enshrined in the Declaration for which the founders fought and died - ideals of law, justice, equality, liberty, and inalienable rights, self-government - are barely understood in America today, much less in the rest of the world.[17] The American Revolution was more than a contest with England. It was and is a war to defend a vision about law, rights, justice, and the God-given dignity of man. The vision was inspired over time by the words of the Bible and the teachings of Christianity but applies to all men everywhere regardless of their faith.[18]

Today, the Declaration's ideas are scoffed at, misrepresented, attacked, ridiculed, held in contempt and ignored. The revolution is not over.

It is important for soldiers and leaders to know that the Declaration stands in the Judeo-Christian stream of political theory. Its legacy must be defended, since it is different both in degree and in kind from its secular counterpart, the French Revolution.[19] This has definite implications for those of us who lead those who pledge to fight and defend the Constitution of the United States against all enemies foreign and domestic.

Even if one does not accept the truth of the Christian faith, prudence argues for the promulgation of its moral code in every area of public life because history has demonstrated that Christian morality is indispensable to the preservation of a free society.[20]

Alexis de Tocqueville in the early part of the 19th century was commissioned by the French government to travel throughout the United States in order to discover the secret of the astounding success of this experiment in democracy. The French were mystified by the conditions of social tranquility and unparalleled freedom present in America. This is what Tocqueville reported: "I do not know whether all Americans have a sincere faith in their religion-for who can know the human heart--but I am certain that they hold it to be indispensable for the maintenance of republican institutions. This opinion is not peculiar to a class of citizens or to a party, but it belongs to the whole rank of society." America, Tocqueville added, is "the place where the Christian religion has kept the greatest power over men's souls; and nothing better demonstrates how useful and natural it is to man, since the country where it now has the widest sway is both the most enlightened and the freest."[21]

John Quincy Adams, America's sixth President, acknowledged

that from the beginning Americans "connected in one indissoluble band the principles of civil government with the principles of Christianity."[22]

The colonists believed in a "Higher Law"-a definite thing that could be found in a particular place, namely the Bible, under whose commandments all would be equally subjected. Samuel Adams, the great revolutionary organizer, in his 1772 classic of political history, The Rights of the Colonists, wrote: "The right of freedom being a gift of God Almighty,...the rights of the colonists as Christians...may be best understood by reading and carefully studying the institutes of the Great Law Giver...which are to be found clearly written and promulgated in the New Testament."[23]

Judges throughout English and American history have often handed down decisions with explicit references to the Ten Commandments, the "Higher Law" handed down by God to show us how to live with each other, how to order their moral lives and their community, and how to please Him. James Madison, known as the father of the U.S. Constitution, put it this way: "We have staked the whole future of the American civilization, not upon the power of government, far from it. We have staked the future...upon the capacity of each and all of us to govern ourselves, to control ourselves, to sustain ourselves according to the Ten Commandments of God."[24]

In 1978, perhaps with some of this history in mind, the Kentucky Legislature required that the Ten Commandments be posted in the public schools along with the following statement: "The secular application as the fundamental legal code of Western civilization and the common law of the United States."[25] But in 1980, the Supreme Court ruled that the posting of the Ten Commandments in Kentucky public schools was a violation of the First Amendment's clause forbidding the establishment of religion. This ruling essentially made it "unconstitutional" for public schools to teach the true origin of America's common law heritage, which undergirds the U.S. Constitution and which is specifically referred to in the Seventh Amendment.[26] Instead of protecting religion from the state, as our founding fathers had intended, we were protecting the state from religion.

This 1980 ruling followed the already astounding 1962 decision banning all religious expression from the public schools. As a result of these rulings, many public schools have dropped "Christmas programs" and carols from their traditional Christmas celebrations. Our courts have misinterpreted what James Madison and Fisher Ames had in mind when they introduced the First Amendment. What was introduced to guarantee "the free exercise" of religion is being used to obliterate religion.

Every President, from George Washington to George Bush, has placed his hand on a Bible and asked for the protection of God upon taking the oath of office. Both Houses of Congress open each daily session with prayer.[27] "In God We Trust" is forever present on our currency. Witnesses in court are expected to swear on the Bible that they will "tell the whole truth and nothing but the truth, so help me God." Each day's session of the Supreme Court is opened with, "God save the United States and the Honorable Court." By ruling of the Supreme Court, the Ten Commandments cannot appear in our schools but appear on the wall above the head of the Chief Justice in the Supreme Court.

Man has a religious nature that he can never escape. The atheists like Madalyn Murray O'Hair and Bertrand Russell, are as religious as Mother Teresa, John Wesley, and Martin Luther.[28] The atheist believes wholeheartedly that God does not exist and that there is no life after death. The theist, on the other hand, believes that God does exist and that one's choices here on earth have a bearing on one's eternal destiny. Most soldiers, when confronted with their own mortality, are theists.

Agnosticism is no less of a faith than Christianity or atheism. The agnostic does not know if God exists, but believes that if God exists, it makes no difference in his life. America has become politically and culturally agnostic, and the Christian faith in the minds of many has come to represent intolerance. The notion of moral absolutes sounds authoritarian and dogmatic even to some Christians.[29] We are offered an alternative in "pluralistic agnosticism", connoting a non-confrontational, live-and-let-live life style. An example is the Supreme Court's abortion ruling which overturned laws in all 50 states and condemned millions of unborn babies to slaughter with a stroke of the pen. The majority opinion states explicitly that "religious belief can have no bearing on how we determine when human life begins." Even William O. Douglas, one of the most liberal Supreme Court justices in

12

history, admitted that "we are a religious people whose institutions presuppose a supreme being."[30] Agnostic pluralism releases man from the constraints placed on him by God and raises man up as the measure of all things.

The real danger is that we are shifting away from the God of Scripture, immutable and unchanging, toward the god of human convenience. Formally, this philosophy is not called pluralism, but secular humanism--the view that man is the sole judge of the world, including morality, the shape of society, and the value of the individual.[31] Those who take stands on Christian doctrines condemning sex outside of marriage, abortion, and homosexuality are quickly labeled and become victims of the American Civil Liberties Union, Planned Parenthood, People for the American Way, abortion rights groups and others.

THE GROWING THREAT - A CRUMBLING HOUSE

^Until about thirty years ago, the name "America" would evoke a feeling of pride, gratitude, and hope. America's moral and fiscal currency was the soundest in the world. We were the free world's policeman; an encouraging older brother to those young nations struggling to achieve democracy: and the hope of all peoples still in bondage.[32] At home we were confident that we were making the world a better place in which to live.

There had been a gradual, sustained improvement that most men could trace in their own lifetimes and the future looked promising. We were technologically superior and breakthroughs were a daily happening. Medically, we were on the verge of conquering every disease known to man.[33] In a word, optimism summed up America.

All of a sudden, everything went out of balance. Our military ventures ceased to go according to plan. We were actually in danger of losing. A president who personified the American dream was assassinated. Young people began to lash out at authority and escape into the "mindless self-destruction of drug abuse".[34] Nations we had helped turned against us with hatred and our foreign policy devolved into one of reaction.

On the home front, our economy became erratic and became a destabilizing factor among the people. Suddenly our children were two years behind the averages of a decade before by college-entrance standards. Mathematics and English aptitudes were plummeting. Industry gave way to services and a greater percentage of the population was on welfare than ever before. Our optimism was turning to despair. In a few short years the public sector ballooned so that it now consumes over one-third of the entire U.S. economy- and most of this has occurred since the ban on prayer in public schools in 1962.[35]

But perhaps the most telling indicator of our condition was the extent of our moral decay. We scrambled to accommodate sexual promiscuity through permissive sex education, more effective and available birth control, and legalized abortion. The family unit was disintegrating, heretofore the thread which kept American fabric together. The divorce rate approached one failed marriage in two, child abuse soared, and parents abdicated their traditional roles of leadership.[36]

Alexis de Tocqueville foresaw the likely consequences of permitting the erosion of America's moral foundations, and predicted that if this occurred, we would see the rise of a new form of despotism, unique to democratic societies; "over its people", he wrote, "will stand an immense, protective power which is alone responsible for securing their enjoyment and watching over their fate... it gladly works for their happiness but wants to be the sole agent and judge of it. It provides for their security, foresees and supplies their necessities, facilitates their pleasures, manages their principal concerns, directs their industry, makes rules for their testaments, and divides their inheritances...Thus, it daily makes the exercise of free choice less useful and more rare, restricts the activity of free will

15

within a more narrow compass, and little by little robs each citizen of the proper use of his own faculties."[37]

We hit the depths of despair when our President, the symbol of all that was right and decent in America, was caught lying to the people and manipulating our trust.

What happened to the American Dream? The truth is that the Dream is turning into a nightmare! Our founding fathers gave us the answer. They knew this nation was founded by God with a special calling. The people who first came here knew that they were being led here by the Lord Jesus Christ, to found a nation where men, women, and children were to live in obedience to Him. This was truly to be "One Nation Under God".

The reason, I believe, that we Americans are in such trouble today is that we have forgotten, rejected, and become cynical about being "Under God". We, as a people, have thrown away our Christian heritage.

The free world is threatened now, not because of lack of resources, but from a spiritual and moral void, which is always accompanied by a corrosion of the will. With religious expression now outlawed from large portions of American public life -in the name of a very distorted civil libertarian creed - can it be long before America goes the way of Greece and Rome of old? Tocqueville had this to say of those who attack faith in God in the name of pluralism:

When such men as these attack religious beliefs, they obey the dictates of their passions, not their interests. Religion is much more needed in the republic they advocate than in the monarchy they attack, and in democratic republics most of all. How could society

16

escape destruction if, when political ties are relaxed, moral ties are not tightened?[38]

Asked Tocqueville: "What will happen to a people master of itself if it is not subject to God?"

History is strewn with the remains of nations, once great, who let the decay from within bring them to ruin. Historians record in the <u>Rise and Fall of the Roman Empire</u> how the Empire rose to greatness. Prosperity, excellence in culture and architecture, discoveries in medicine were but a few of the reasons its citizens assumed that the Empire would be around for centuries to come. Greek civilization rose to its "Golden Age" and gave the world its first historical attempt at democracy. Soon corruption set in and infiltrated every aspect of Greek life - even religion. In time Greece fell, and with it democracy, because it lacked the moral fiber and spiritual leadership to undergird it.

Other great civilizations have come and gone as corruption took hold. Today they are merely ghosts of the past with little to show for their great achievements and victories.

Does the same black shadow already loom over America? Civilizations do not just die. Their leaders and people are first deceived; then they are destroyed by God. Ephesians 5:6 says, "Let no man deceive you with vain words: for because of these things (immorality, covetousness, worship of false gods, etc.) cometh the wrath of God upon the children of disobedience." Do we already believe "the lie" that was first given to Eve in the garden of Eden: "...ye shall be as gods, knowing (deciding for yourselves) good and evil" (Gen 3:5)?

17

When a nation listens to "the lie" it dethrones God and deifies man's achievements. It exalts human reason as supreme. It trusts education and science to solve its problems. It believes that man is evolving into perfection. It replaces God's moral standards with situational ethics. It promotes sensual pleasure and instant gratification. It strives for a world utopia of prosperity and peace. It makes the State the sovereign dictator over everyone.[39]

Rome believed the lie. Man became the measure of all things. The human body was idolized. Only the strong survived. "Rome was quite tolerant of all religions except Christianity. Christianity was banned and Christians were persecuted, burned, and thrown to the lions."[40] Why? Because the very nature of Christianity is contrary to the lie that man and the human mind are supreme, the basis of every other religion.

America is in danger and the greatest threat to our national security is from within. We may feel invincible and destined to lead the world for decades to come but already we are exhibiting characteristics of civilizations that have disintegrated and disappeared.

Fortunately, many are alert to the impending danger. They are calling America to wake up and resume our rightful position as a "Nation Under God". The survival of our nation and our Army depends on it.

Spiritual strength begins with individual faith. Our hope lies in the promise that God made to Israel when she was an infant

nation realizing that she would drift towards believing "the lie".
"If my people which are called by my name will humble themselves
and pray and seek My face and turn from their wicked ways, then I
will hear from Heaven and will forgive their sin and heal their
land" (2 Chron. 7:14).

On April 30th, 1863, President Abraham Lincoln called for a
National Day of Fasting, Humiliation and Prayer.

We have been the recipients of the choicest bounties of heaven. We
have been preserved, these many years, in peace and prosperity. We
have grown in numbers, wealth and power, as no other nation has
ever grown. But we have forgotten God. We have forgotten the
gracious hand which preserved us in peace, and multiplied and
enriched and strengthened us; and we have vainly imagined, in the
deceitfulness of our hearts, that all these blessings were produced
by some superior wisdom and virtue of our own. Intoxicated with
unbroken success, we have become too self-sufficient to feel the
necessity of redeeming and preserving grace, too proud to pray to
the God that made us! It behooves us, then to humble ourselves
before the offended Power, to confess our national sins, and to
pray for clemency and forgiveness.

President Lincoln clearly understood that the nation needed to
turn back to God, to commit to Him, and to begin rebuilding the
spiritual foundations that had been crumbling. What Lincoln
understood in 1863 is even more clearly seen today - the growing
threat to America - the house crumbles from within.

Before his death, Thomas Jefferson also saw the inevitable
result of continuing in our present direction. He said, "Indeed,
I tremble for my country when I reflect that God is just, and that
His justice cannot sleep forever."[41]

The spiritual strength of our nation will determine the
strength of our armed forces. Personal faith and spiritual
strength are key to a soldier's ability to function under combat

stress.   Just as we cannot afford to neglect the spiritual condition of our nation we must realize that the success of our Army on any future battlefield will to a great extent depend on the spiritual condition of our soldiers.

SOLDIERING - THE SPIRITUAL DIMENSION

Modern historians have come to realize that the first key to understanding any armed force is to realize that it is an extension of the society that created it. A corollary is that an armed force is likely to be no stronger than the society it serves.

With the erosion of a nation's religious life, we inevitably find a dissipation of the will. Americans have lost sight of the fact that a price must be paid for freedom. The preservation of liberty sometimes involves personal sacrifice. Americans in the past have believed that there are certain values more precious that life itself, and one of those is freedom.

Ancient Greece ultimately collapsed because the Greek philosophy never provided individuals a rationale for making sacrifices in defense of principle. The perpetuation of the state, or even of the society, was not, in the final analysis, reason enough to lay down one's life. The average Athenian felt a sense of isolation, rootlessness, and that he was living a life without purpose. Athenian soldiers' will to fight and defend the state deteriorated with the will of the people. Ancient Greece imploded into a spiritual abyss before it was defeated by the Macedonians in the fourth century B.C.

Perceptive leaders recognize the significance of faith and spiritual strength to sustain soldiers in battle. Soldiers with combat experience have confirmed that judgement.

General George C. Marshall said,

I look upon the spiritual life of the soldier as even more important than his physical equipment...The soldier's heart, the

soldier's spirit, the soldier's soul are everything. Unless the
soldier's soul sustains him, he cannot be relied upon and will fail
himself and his country in the end. It's morale--and I mean
spiritual morale--which wins victory in the ultimate, and that type
of morale can only come out of the religious nature of the soldier
who knows God and who has the spirit of religious fervor in his
soul. I count heavily on that type of man and that kind of Army.[42]

Why do American soldiers fight? Are we equipping them
properly? In considering these questions, Samuel Stouffer in The
American Soldier: Combat and its Aftermath, investigated the
motivational factors that increased the soldier's resources for
enduring combat stress.[43] As a result of an extensive survey he
found that faith in God and prayer were crucial to enduring combat
stress for the majority of soldiers.

The only other item approaching prayer in the proportion of men who
said it helped them a lot was thinking that "you couldn't let the
other men down"--touching on potent forces of group solidarity and
loyalty--but in both theaters (European and Pacific) more of the
men, regardless of educational level or of whether they were
privates or noncoms, said that prayer was helpful.[44]

Stouffer noted that men with combat experience were "more
likely than men who did not see combat to agree that their Army
experiences had increased their faith in God."[45] He found that 79%
of WW II combat veterans reported increased faith in God.

Military historians and theorists have long recognized the
influence of personal faith and spiritual strength on the soldier's
ability to function under combat stress. Success on any future
battlefield will depend upon the spiritual condition of our
soldiers.

In describing the actions of his unit during an ambush in
Vietnam, an American soldier said, "We all asked the help of the

22

Lord that night."[46]

My experience during seven months in Saudi Arabia for DESERT SHIELD/DESERT STORM is that even the hardest, most irreligious appearing soldiers find time to pray when confronted with death and their own mortality.

When the Second Continental Congress gathered on May 10, 1775 under the leadership of John Hancock, they were looking for the one man who could lead them to victory over a mother country who was determined to suppress the "revolt". They needed someone who could transform a part-time militia of farmers, merchants, and preachers into a disciplined army. John Adams proposed George Washington as the obvious choice. On June 15, he was unanimously selected to lead America into war. He said he would accept the command only on the condition that Congress appoint and fund chaplains for his troops, which Congress promptly did.[47]

Washington was a committed and believing Christian who preferred a more private religious life marked by a living faith.[48] Historians have avoided discussing Washington's religious life yet it can be seen that he was a devout Christian by looking at his private prayer book written in his own handwriting. The very first entry in the Daily Sacrifice reads as follows:

Almighty God, and most merciful Father, who didst command the children of Israel to offer a daily sacrifice to Thee, that thereby they might glorify and praise Thee for Thy protection both night and day...I beseech Thee, my sins, remove them from Thy presence, as far as the east is from the west, and accept of me for the merits of Thy Son Jesus Christ... Let my heart, therefore, gracious God, be so affected with the glory and majesty of (Thine honor) that I may not do mine own works, but wait on Thee...As Thou wouldst hear me calling upon Thee in my prayers, so give me grace to hear Thee calling on me in Thy word, that it may be wisdom, righteousness, reconciliation and peace to the saving of my soul in the day of the Lord Jesus.

His second entry written at the close of the day reflects acknowledgement of who God is:

O most glorious God, in Jesus Christ...I acknowledge and confess my faults, in the weak and imperfect performance of the duties of this day. I have called on Thee for pardon and forgiveness of sins, but so coldly and carelessly that my prayers are become my sin and stand in need of pardon. I have heard Thy holy word, but with such deadness of spirit that I have been an unprofitable and forgetful hearer... Let me live according to those holy rules which Thou hast this day prescribed in Thy holy word...Direct me to the true object, Jesus Christ the way, the truth and the life. Bless, O Lord, all the people of this land.[49]

General Washington clearly understood the spiritual dimension of soldiering as it applied to his own life and the life of those he was to lead. It was no mistake he was chosen to lead the Continental Army. That Army has become the standard, the spiritual yardstick that others are measured against. MG Barry R. McCaffrey, in an address to the Army War College on 14 August 1991, stated that, "the DESERT STORM Army was made up of the most religious soldiers since [Washington's] army of Northern Virginia." Yet my experience in DESERT STORM elicits a different observation. The DESERT STORM Army that I observed had only a very small percentage of soldiers who brought a personal faith with them to the desert. What did surface after deployment was a greater sensitivity to spiritual things among soldiers. Many of those who struggled with life in the desert, priorities, loneliness, family separations and their own mortality sought answers to life's tough questions. When confronted with their own lack of control over their destiny and circumstances (the basis for "secular humanism") many turned to

24

God. Some found new life in Jesus Christ as He became the answer to the tough questions. This confirmed the old adage that "there are no foxhole atheists". Very few leaders had considered the spiritual dimension of soldiering and the role of faith in sustaining the soldier prior to deployment. Consequently, both leaders and soldiers were not equipped. The months before combat did provide some time to "train" on spiritual things but we fell far short because of the years of neglect. Spiritually, today's Army falls far short of the Continental Army. The soldier, on the other hand, has a hunger for spiritual things that is accentuated when in crisis.

Washington put a premium on the spiritual training and equipping of his soldiers because he understood the possible hardships his army was to undergo and the sustaining nature of faith.

In 1985, speaking at Fort Monmouth, New Jersey, General John W. Vessey, Jr., said, "The spiritual health of the Armed Forces is as important as the physical health of its members or the condition of its equipment."[50] General Vessey's statement was rooted in experience and reflected years of observing soldiers in and out of combat. He demonstrates a keen awareness of the need for spiritual training and leadership to insure spiritual health.

Clausewitz "is widely acclaimed for having broken with the sterile material-oriented theories of the 17th and 18th centuries and for having brought the human, moral and psychological factor back into the theory of war."[51] In recent times, more and more leaders have become aware that faith and spiritual well-being are important in the lives of soldiers and their families.

The importance of faith in a combat environment is well documented. There are striking instances where faith and the spirit that resulted enabled a small number of soldiers to have a far greater impact than anyone could imagine. The defense of Little Round Top at the battle of Gettysburg was just such an instance. The 20th Maine-three hundred and fifty strong, commanded by Colonel Joshua Chamberlain, minister of the gospel of Jesus Christ and college professor, held their defensive position against overwhelming odds. The attackers remarked that the defenders had no fear, as if they already knew the outcome.[52]

Faith can supply hope because we know we are not alone and because God knows the outcome. Jesus Christ tells us that He will never leave us or forsake us. It is our hope in His promises and in Him that enables us to stand firm in the face of overwhelming odds. Hope is needed to dispel the fear that can immobilize even the fiercest warrior. Whereas fear can make one visualize the worst in everything, faith gives us hope for the best and a peace about the future.

Faith links us to values worth fighting for, sacrificing for, dying for. During a crisis we tend to more closely examine our lives and that which is important. People who experience tragedy in their lives will tell you that it reorders their priorities.

Leaders must be as capable of evaluating the moral and spiritual fitness of the soldiers in their units as they are of evaluating physical fitness or technical competence.

SPIRITUAL LEADERSHIP

When Washington took command of the Continental Army at Cambridge on July 2, he immediately sent out an order forbidding "profane swearing, cursing and drunkenness. And in like manner," the order stated, "he [Washington] requires and expects of all officers and soldiers, not engaged in actual duty, a punctual attendance of Divine services, to implore the blessing of Heaven upon the means used for our safety and defense."[53] He also added that a national day of fasting on July 20 would be "religiously observed by the forces under his command exactly in the manner directed by the Continental Congress." Moreover, said Washington's order, "it is expected that all those who go to worship do take their arms, ammunition and accoutrements, and are prepared for immediate action if called upon."[54]

General Washington was a man of deep personal faith and clearly understood the spiritual dimension of soldiering. He believed that "there would not have been a Revolutionary victory and the birth of a new nation without God's intervention and blessing."[55] Moreover, his soldiers understood and accepted his spiritual leadership. That, combined with his presence and constant example, gave them strength to endure incredible hardships and defeat a better equipped enemy. The Continental Army was clearly a reflection of the society which it served. The society was God fearing, upright, enduring, and understood the need to be under authority--first of God and then of those appointed over them.

Even though the Army has provided chaplains for our units for over two hundred years, very little has been said about the spiritual role of the leader. While our literature is replete with material focusing on competencies and characteristics essential for leaders, spiritual faith and the spiritual requirements of our leaders are seldom addressed. Leaders of our nation and our nation's soldiers need to know the importance of spiritual leadership, a role they cannot abdicate. Even Clausewitz recognized the importance of intellectual, moral, and spiritual strength in superior nations and armed forces. He stated that all military action is "intertwined with geistige," intellectual and spiritual forces and effects.[56] He was concerned that military theory not ignore "these subjective forces which are precisely most decisive" when studying warfare.[57]

The great task ahead must be to return to first principles, principles upon which America's founders were in overwhelming agreement. They were firmly convinced that liberty was essential to happiness and prosperity in this world; that constitutional government was essential to liberty; that the preservation of both was contingent on Christian morality which could not long stand without firm faith in Christ. As Tocqueville wrote: "Liberty regards religion as its companion in all its battles and triumphs, as the cradle of its infancy and the divine source of its claims."

FM 22-100 states that, "What you are (your beliefs, values, ethics, and character) is the most important part of your leadership.[58]

In his book entitled <u>Leadership</u>, James Mac Gregor Burns states,

...moral leadership concerns him the most...moral leadership is not mere preaching, or the uttering of pieties, or the insistence on social conformity...but emerges from, and always returns to the fundamental wants and needs, aspirations, and values of the followers...the kind of leadership that can produce social change that will satisfy follower's authentic needs.[59]

In his book, <u>The Closing of the American Mind</u>, Allan Bloom looks at American higher education and concludes that man longs for something we have lost--the kind of substance that gave meaning to the Declaration of Independence in which men pledged "their lives, their fortunes, and their sacred honor".[60] Bloom points out that in years past students arrived at the University already possessing an educational heritage rooted in the Bible, the family, and the American political tradition centered on the Declaration of Independence--"The Bible was the common culture, one that united the simple and the sophisticated, rich and poor, young and old".[61]

General of the Army Omar Bradley made these comments after WWII,

With the monstrous weapons man already has, humanity is in danger of being trapped in this world by its moral adolescents. Our knowledge of science has clearly outstripped our capacity to control it. We have many men of science; too few men of God. We have grasped the mystery of the atom and rejected the Sermon on the Mount. Man is stumbling blindly through a spiritual darkness while toying with the precarious secrets of life and death. The world has achieved brilliance without wisdom, power without conscience. Ours is a world of nuclear giants and ethical infants. We know more about war than we know about peace, more about killing than we know about living. This is our 20th Century's claim to distinction and to progress.[62]

We are in danger as a Nation and an Army. As we move toward secular humanism and relativism there is a frightening possibility

30

that we will lose God's blessing, the Spirit of America, and our fighting spirit as soldiers.

The soldier is spiritually hungry. Chaplain (Col) David Peterson, Central Command Staff Chaplain for DESERT SHIELD/DESERT STORM said that commanders and senior NCO's had underestimated the spiritual interests and needs of their soldiers in the desert.[63] Leaders at every level sensed a personal requirement to actively support their soldiers spiritually and meet their spiritual needs.

Many leaders found themselves ill equipped to meet this need because of their lack of personal faith and spiritual training. They were good at military training and equipping the soldiers tactically but rarely considered the spiritual climate of their unit to be an important part of the command climate. In many units the term "combat ready" not only meant training hardened soldiers but a "hardness" evidenced by hard talk, hard drinking, and hard--immoral--living. In Southwest Asia, commanders discovered a new dimension to combat readiness--faith. They discovered that the "moral/spiritual fibre of the soldier is an absolutely, critically important part of being ready for the ultimate mission."[64]

Leaders cannot ignore the soldier's need for spiritual training and the need to see model spiritual leaders any more than they can ignore tough, demanding field training, leadership development and leadership by example. Spiritual leadership is critical to our Nation and our Army. This type of leadership is provided by those who have a strong personal faith, a leadership style based on Biblical principles, and have developed the proper spiritual climate in their units and organizations. When leaders put a premium on the value of being "Under God" then there is hope. We dare not take anything for granted.

A Strong Personal Faith

Spiritual leadership can be exercised only by Spirit-filled men and women. One must be personally "Under God" before he can hope to bring his unit "Under God". However brilliant a man may be intellectually, however capable an administrator, without a personal relationship with Jesus Christ, he is incapable of giving truly spiritual leadership. "Reduced to its simplest terms, to be filled with the Spirit means that, through voluntary surrender and in response to appropriating faith, the human personality is filled, mastered, controlled by the Holy Spirit."[65] Under the Spirit's control, natural gifts of leadership are refined and sanctified (used God's way).

The reason personal faith is so important is that it provides the foundation for who we are and how we lead. It is impossible to understand God's plan without it. With faith goes accountability and conformance. Ultimately we are accountable to God for our actions. Our concern should be whether or not our actions accentuate that which is against God. We are to be conformed to the image of His Son, Jesus Christ. From Him we see the master principle for leadership--servanthood. The contrast between the world's idea of leadership and that of Christ is brought into sharp focus in Mark 10:42-43: "You know that those who are recognized as

32

rulers of the Gentiles lord it over them; and their great men exercise authority over them. But it is not so among you. But whoever wishes to be first among you shall be slave of all."

It is a general principle that we can lead and influence others only so far as we ourselves have gone. "The person most likely to be successful is one who leads not by merely pointing the way but by having trodden it himself."[66] The same is true when considering the spiritual dimension of leadership. We are leaders to the extent that others are inspired to follow us. Only by believing in the need for a personal faith ourselves will we be able to encourage those we lead to develop their personal faith.

A Leadership Style Based on Biblical Principles

"Leadership is influence, the ability of one person to influence others. One can lead only to the extent that he can influence them to follow his lead."[67] Spiritual leadership is a blending of natural and spiritual qualities. Even the natural qualities are God-given and can only reach their highest effectiveness when employed in His service--"Under God."

In his book, Spiritual Leadership, J. Oswald Sanders compares some of the dominant characteristics of natural and spiritual leadership. While they have many points of similarity, they also have many points of dissimilarity.

[68]Natural	Spiritual
Self-confident	Confident in God
Knows men	Also knows God

33

Makes own decisions	Seeks to find God's will
Ambitious	Self-effacing
Originates own methods	Follows God's methods
Enjoys commanding others	Delights to obey God
Independent	God-dependent

Are Biblical qualities of leadership compatible with leading soldiers? The answer is a resounding "YES". Judge for yourself as you compare the following, essential, Biblical leadership qualities with what you would desire in your subordinate leaders.

Great leaders, both natural and spiritual, have always been great encouragers. In these days of discouragement and disillusionment, this trait is even more crucial. We all should lean toward encouragement-slanted leadership. Hebrews 10:25 exhorts us--"Let us encourage one another, and all the more, as you see the day drawing near."

Leaders must be disciplined. They are able to lead because they have conquered themselves. Many are unable to lead because they have never learned to follow. They have never learned to be accountable and practice good followership. Generally others are willing to accept the discipline and follow a strongly disciplined leader more readily and cooperatively. He has set an example to be copied and conformed to. Leaders under the authority of God understand followership and discipline.

Men of faith have vision, for faith is vision. Vision includes foresight and insight and includes both optimism and hope.

34

"No pessimist ever made a great leader."[69] This vision sees through the eyes of an optimist who sees an opportunity in every difficulty and sees God's hand working to refine, restructure and redirect. He can see good coming from bad because his trust in the only one who sees the future--God.

Decisive action characterizes a spirit-led leader. When in the will of God, one can press on, regardless of the consequences. The vision that comes through faith demands decisive action. We must do something about what we have seen and heard. Procrastination and vacillation can be fatal to good leadership.

In reply to a question, a prominent business man said, "If I had to name the one most important quality of a top manager, I would say, 'personal integrity' -sincere in promise, faithful in discharge of duty, upright in finances, loyal in service, honest in speech."[70] The quality of personal integrity would probably be on everyone's list-maybe at the top. Ultimately our integrity is based on "to whom we are responsible". If one is accountable to God then they must be reminded that there is no time or place that escapes His scrutiny. Crucial to this quality is ones ability to honestly admit mistakes and shortcomings.

One quality that many of our leaders lack is courage. It takes courage to take the harder right rather than the easier wrong. It takes courage to follow your convictions in light of severe peer pressure and opposition. "The couraye of a leader is demonstrated in his being willing to face unpleasant and even devastating facts and conditions with equanimity and then acting

35

with firmness in the light of them, even though it means incurring personal unpopularity."[71] Faith enables us to have courage in our convictions and to realize that God's ways are worth pursuing in the face of adversity.

Webster's dictionary defines our next quality, <u>wisdom</u>, as "the faculty of making the use of knowledge, a combination of discernment, judgement, sagacity and similar powers. In scripture, wisdom refers to right judgment concerning spiritual and moral truth. Wisdom takes into account people's experiences, weaknesses, and strengths. It involves the knowledge of God with insight into man's heart. It is the right application of knowledge in situations where the solution is not obvious. With wisdom goes understanding.

The final quality to be discussed is <u>peace</u>. Most "leadership lists" would not include this quality although it is essential to effective, spiritual leadership. It takes peace to be a good leader. Of the years of recorded civilization, very few have been without war. This is true with individuals too. How few people live a life that is calm and free from anxiety. The Jewish word "Shalom" means peace--"keeping your mind firmly fixed on God" and adjusting your life accordingly. Peace comes from trust which comes from faith. Totally trusting God gives peace. The leader that possesses this quality will be more tolerant, calm, relaxed, patient, less concerned about himself--at peace.

Spiritual Climate

Command climate provides the environment in which the job gets done. A major sub-climate and emphasis area within the command climate must be spiritual climate. To what degree is it acceptable to be a person of faith within this unit? Is it encouraged and modeled? Is it more acceptable than "living in the fast lane"? Is going to church and being in Bible study the rule rather than the exception? Does peer pressure encourage deviate behavior or bring out the best of the spiritual dimension of the soldier? Are we helping turn America back to a Nation "Under God" by encouraging our soldiers to find spiritual roots? All these questions reflect on the spiritual climate.

Religious support is a charge given to the Unit Ministry Team (UMT), the chaplain and his or her enlisted assistant, by doctrine. Many commanders fail to realize that there is a difference between command responsibility and support. Consequently, many commanders and leaders abdicate their rightful role in the spiritual development of their units. The UMTs assist the commander--it is the commander's responsibility. This is one responsibility that cannot be delegated because the commander and senior nco's determine the spiritual climate. The mere act of delegating one's spiritual responsibility reveals the level of importance placed on spiritual development.

The mission of the UMT was described in the Army Trainer by a maneuver analyst for the Army's Combined Arms Training Activity, Fort Leavenworth, Kansas as follows:

The UMT's mission on the Airland battlefield is to provide comprehensive religious, moral, and spiritual support to soldiers

37

and their units. The UMT assists the commander by facilitating spiritual factors that enable soldiers to strengthen their faith. Thereby they achieve inner stability and peace. Inner strength reinforces the bond among soldiers and enhances both individual and group spiritual awareness. A proactive UMT fosters unit cohesion; this ultimately encourages high motivation, thorough dedication, and effective performance among its members.[72]

Army doctrine states that: Chaplains and chaplain assistants are normally assigned on a one-to-one basis. In smaller units chaplain section is comprised of one chaplain and one chaplain assistant who together constitute the "Unit Ministry Team [UMT]."[73] Units with healthy spiritual climates within their command climate would say the Unit Ministry Team consists of the commander, the chaplain, and the chaplain's assistant. The commander alone is the single most important factor in establishing the spiritual climate.

Strong spiritual climates within organizations are characterized as having commander involvement, providing freedom of ministry action for the UMT, allocating time and training resources, and being open to spiritual organizations that assist in the spiritual development of the soldier.

The UMT is a tremendous resource but not an end in itself. Combat can shake the underpinnings of life and the UMT is essential to the unit's ability to handle crisis situations. Chaplains must share the soldiers' world and be in constant contact. Many soldiers have no religious foundation and their backgrounds have immunized them against hope. Pastoral care and counseling are invaluable under these conditions. Others seek meaning and faith. Many question religious beliefs and wonder why God let them down. The UMT must be free to minister.

We cannot merely talk of "command support" if we are to have the proper spiritual climate and effective unit ministry. We need to talk of "command involvement".

Our hope for the future is that the Nation's and the Army's leadership will accept their spiritual responsibilities and put a premium on spiritual readiness. Those who have a strong personal faith, lead by example based on Biblical principles and have set the proper spiritual climate will be the ones who turn us back toward being "One Nation Under God".

CONCLUSION

This is a time for spiritual renewal in America. There is hope. We can emerge stronger than before if we will rediscover the foundational truths behind the success of our nation and our Army.

In his farewell address at West Point in 1962, General of the Army Douglas MacArthur spoke eloquently of "the crash of guns, the rattle of musketry, the strange, mournful mutter of the battlefield." He also spoke of the faith that sustains soldiers in combat:

The soldier, above all other men, is required to practice the greatest art of religious training--sacrifice. In battle and in the face of danger and death, he discloses those divine attributes which his Maker gave when he created man in His own image. No physical courage and no brute instinct can take the place of the Divine help which alone can sustain him.[74]

Faith is critical. We must stem the spiritual decay in America. It will take leadership that acknowledges and obeys God's plan.

We need to once again become a "Nation Under God" led by men and women of faith who exhibit spiritual leadership and set a proper spiritual climate. Then and only then will we begin to turn away from relativism and secular humanism and turn back to God.

Leaders are responsible. We cannot turn over our responsibilities of spiritual leadership to the church or our chaplains. The strength of our nation and the effectiveness of our fighting forces depend on leaders that are spiritually responsible.

Great leaders are like eagles. They don't flock--one finds

them one at a time. Leaders like our founding fathers are the rarest of eagles. America's founding fathers understood very well the principle that faith and freedom go together, and that one cannot survive long without the other. Their faith and strength of commitment are well documented. It is for each of us to decide the commitment we are willing to make. It will be for future generations to decide how well the commitment has been honored. The question for each of us is: In my lifetime, did I make a difference in the spiritual renewal of America? Our very existence depends on it!

> THE MIGHTY EAGLE...when his mighty wing feathers become heavy with oil and dirt and his beak and talons become calcified and brittle he retires for a period of renewal...He pulls out his feathers, extracts each claw and smashes his beak against rocks until it is gone...When his beak, talons and feathers have regrown he emerges in a renewed condition--stronger than before...[75]
>
> Be an EAGLE!!

ENDNOTES

1.   Nancy L. DeMoss, <u>The Rebirth of America</u> (Arthur S. DeMoss Foundation, 1986), 75.

2.   Ibid.

3.   Russell F. Weigley. <u>New Dimensions in Military History</u> (California: Presidio Press, 1975), 38-72.

4.   Parker C. Thompson, <u>The United States Army Chaplaincy--From Its European Antecedents to 1791</u> (Washington, 1978), 106.

5.   Ibid., 175.

6.   Gary T. Amos, <u>Defending the Declaration</u> (Tennessee: Wolgemuth and Hyatt Publishers, 1989), 32.

7.   Verna Hall, <u>The Christian History of the Constitution of the United States of America</u> (New York: Human Science Press, 1976), 27.

8.   Hart, 283.

9.   Maurice W. Cranston, <u>John Locke: A Biography</u> (London: Oxford Press, 1957).

10. Ibid., 75.

11. Benjamin Hart. <u>Faith & Freedom</u>. (Texas: Lewis and Stanley Publishers, 1988), 14.

12. Ibid., 78.

13. Ibid., 79.

14. Richard Tuck, <u>Natural Rights Theories: Their Origin and Development</u> (Cambridge: Cambridge University Press, 1979), 1-2.

15. Ibid.

16. Ibid.

17. Amos, 169.

18. Ibid.

19. Ibid., 170.

20. Hart., 15.

21. Alexis De Tocqueville. <u>Democracy in America</u> (New York: 1966).

22. Hart., 16.

23. Hart., 16.

24. Ibid.

25. Ibid., 18.

26. Ibid.

27. Ibid., 19.

28. Ibid.

29. Ibid., 20.

30. Ibid., 21.

31. Ibid., 22.

32. Peter Marshall and David Manuel, <u>The Light and the Glory</u> (Old Tappan, N.J.:Fleming H. Revell Company), 13.

33. Ibid.

34. Ibid.

35. Hart., 24.

36. Ibid., 14.

37. Tocqueville., 155.

38. Ibid.

39. From "Be Alert to Spiritual Danger". (Chicago: Institute of Basic Youth Conflicts, 1979). 17.

40. Ibid.

41. John Price, <u>America at the Crossroads</u> (New York: Tyndale House, 1979), 12.

42. Cited in Daniel B. Jorgensen, <u>The Service of Chaplains to Army Air Units 1917-1946</u>. 277.

43. Samuel A. Stouffer, et al., <u>The American Soldier: Combat and its Aftermath. Studies in Social Psychology in World War II</u>. Vol II, 172.

44.   Ibid., 173.

45.   Ibid., 186.

46.   John Keegan and Richard Holmes, <u>Soldiers: A History of Men in Battle</u> (New York: Viking Press, 1986), 52.

47.   Hart., 273.

48.   Ibid., 274.

49.   William J. Johnson, <u>George Washington, the Christian</u>, (Nashville, Tennessee: 1919), 55.

50.   General John W. Vessey, Jr., Chairman, Joint Chiefs of Staff, from an address for the Anniversary of the Chaplain Branch given at the U.S. Army Chaplain Center and School, Fort Monmouth, NJ, 29 July 1985.

51.   Jurg Martin Gabriel, <u>Clausewitz Revisited; a Study of His Writings and of the Debate Over Their Relevance to Deterrence Theory</u>. 48.

52.   Keegan and Holmes, 48.

53.   Ibid.

54.   Ibid.

55.   John Schumacher. Address given at the Baccalaureate service at the Sergeants Major Academy, 1 July 1991. "The Spiritual Dimension of Leadership."

56.   Peter Paret, <u>Clausewitz and the State</u>. (New York: Oxford Press, 1976), 85.

57.   Ibid.

58.   FM 22-100., 24.

59.   James Mac Gregor Burns. <u>Leadership</u> (New York: Harper and Row, 1987), 4.

60.   Schumacher.

61.   Ibid.

62.   Omar M. Bradley.

63.   Schumacher.

64.   Ibid.

65. J. Oswald Sanders. <u>Spiritual Leadership</u> (Chicago: Moody Press, 1986). 101.

66. Ibid., 37.

67. Ibid., 35.

68. Ibid., 38.

69. Ibid., 73.

70. Ibid., 82.

71. Ibid., 79.

72. Timothy R. Dicker, Cpt, "On the Battlefield: Stress, Fatigue, Fear", <u>Army Trainer</u>. 13.

73. U.S. Army Combat Developments Command, <u>The Chaplain's Role as Related to Soldier Motivation</u>. 2-3.

74. Douglas MacArthur, Address to the members of the Association of Graduates, United States Military Academy at West Point, New York, 12 May 1962.

75. Cited from Betty Spooner, 1982. "The Eagle".

BIBLIOGRAPHY

Adams, Charles Francis, ed. The Works of John Adams. 10 vols. Boston: Charles C. Little and James Brown, 1850.

Adams, John. The Political Writings of John Adams. Indianapolis: 1954.

Ahlstrom, Sydney E. A Religious History of the American People. New Haven: Yale University Press. 1972.

Alexander, Bevin. Korea: The First War We Lost. New York: Hippocrene Books, 1986.

Alley, Robert S., ed. James Madison on Religious Liberty. Buffalo, NY: Prometheus Books, 1985.

Allison, Andrew M. Thomas Jefferson: Champion of Liberty, A History Of His Life. American Classic Series. Vol 1. Washington, D.C.: National Center for Constitutional Studies, 1983.

American Heritage Dictionary, 1970 ed.

Amos, Gary T. Defending the Declaration. Tennessee: Wolgemuth & Hyatt, 1989.

Andrist, Ralph K., ed. George Washington: A Biography in His Own Words. New York: 1972.

Bailyn, Bernard. The Ideological Origins of the American Revolution. Cambridge, Mass.: Belknap Press, 1982.

Bancroft, George. History of the United States. 10 vols. Boston: University Press, 1838.

Becker, Carl. The Declaration of Independence: A study in the History of Political Ideas. New York: Vintage Books, 1958.

Beoloff, Max. Thomas Jefferson and American Democracy. London: 1965.

Berman, Harold J. Law and Revolution: The Formation of the Western Legal Tradition. Cambridge, Mass.: Harvard University Press, 1983.

Blodgett, David S., "What Change Can Do for an Army." Military Review. Vol. LXVII (3), March 1987, 14-27.

Boorstin, Daniel J. The Americans: The Colonial Experience. New York: Vintage Books 1958.

Bowan, Catherine Drinker. _Miracle at Philadelphia: The Story of the Constitutional Convention, May to September 1787_. Boston: University press, 1966.

Breland, Don C., Chaplain. _The Commander's Perspective on the Role of the Chaplain_. Study Project. Carlisle Barracks: U.S. Army War College, 23 March 1987.

Brown, William Y. _The Army Chaplain: His Office, Duties, and Responsibilities_. Philadelphia: william S. & Alfred Martien, 1963.

Bruce, F.F. _The Letter of Paul to the Romans: An Introduction and Commentary_. 2e ed. vol. 6, The Tyndale New Testament Commentaries. Leon Morris, gen ed. Grand Rapids: William B. Eerdmans, 1985.

Buckingham, Clay T. "Ethics and the Senior Officer: Institutional Tensions." Parameters, Vol. 15. Autumn 1985, 23-32.

Bunyan, John. _Pilgrim's Progress_. Many editions. 1678.

Cappon, Lester J., ed. _The Adams-Jefferson Letters_. 2 vols. Chapel Hill: University of North Carolina Press, 1959.

Carson, Clarence B. _The Rebirth of Liberty: The Founding of the American Republic, 1760-1800_. New Rochelle, NY: Arlington House, 1973.

Chadwick, Owen. _The Reformation_. London: 1968.

Clausewitz, Carl von. _On War_. Ed. and Trans. Michael Howard and Peter Paret. Princeton: Princeton University Press, 1984.

Collins, J. Lawton, GEN. _Army and Navy Journal_. 13 May 1950, 988.

Conkin, Paul. _Self-Evident Truths_. Bloomington: Indiana University Press, 1974.

Cord, Robert L. _Separation of Church and State_. New York: Arlington House, 1982.

Corwin, Edward S. _The "Higher Law" Background of American Constitutional Law_. Ithaca, New York: 1957.

Cranston, Maurice W. _John Locke: A Biography_. London: 1957.

De Tocqueville, Alexis. _Democracy in America_. new York, 1966.

Ebenstein, William. _Great Political Thinkers: Plato to the Present_. Hinsdale, Ill.: Dryden Press, 1969.

Eisenhower, Dwight D., GEN. _Circular Letter_. No. 310, 1 July

1946, 3.

Erikson, Erik H. <u>Identity: Youth and Crisis</u>. New York: W.W. Norton, 1968.

Figley, C.R., ed. <u>Stress Disorders of Vietnam Veterans: Theory, Research and Treatment</u>. New York: Brenner/Mazel, 1978.

Flexner, James Thomas. <u>George Washington</u>. 4 vols. Boston: University Press, 1965-72.

Ford, Paul Leicester, ed. <u>The Writings of Thomas Jefferson</u>. 10 Vols. New York: G.P. Putnam's Sons, 1892.

Fowler, James. <u>Stages of Faith: The Psychology of Human Development and the Quest for Meaning</u>. New york: Harper and Row, 1981.

Frankl, Viktor E. <u>Man's Search for Meaning</u>. New York: Pocket Books edition, 1974.

Fromm, Erich. <u>The Revolution of Hope</u>. New York: Harper and Row, 1968.

Gallup, George, Jr., and Poling, David. <u>The Search for America's Faith</u>. Nashville, Tennessee: Abingdon Press, 1980.

Garraty, John A. <u>The American Nation: A History of the United States to 1877</u>. 5th ed. New York: Harper and Row, 1983.

Gaustad, Edwin S. <u>Faith of Our Fathers: Religion and the New Nation</u>. San Francisco: Harper and Row, 1987.

Goldberg, George. <u>Church, State and the Constitution: The Religion Clause Upside Down</u>. Washington, D.C.: 1984. Account of how modern court rulings have reversed the original intent of the First Amendment.

Goodrich, Charles A. <u>Lives of the Signers of the Declaration of Independence</u>. 4th ed. Boston: Thomas Mather, 1834.

Grinker, Ray and Siegel, John P.1 <u>Men Under Stress</u>. Blakiston Press, 1943.

Hall, Thomas C. <u>The Religious Background of American Culture</u>. Boston: University Press, 1930. A study of the pervasive influence of Puritan ideas on American life and thought.

Hall, Verna N., ed. <u>The Christian History of the Constitution of the United States of America</u>. San Francisco: 1962 and 1966. Compilation of original documents.

Hansell, Norris. <u>The Person in Distress</u>. New York: Human Science Press, 1976.

Hart, Benjamin. <u>Faith & Freedom</u>. Texas: Lewis and Stanley Publishers, 1988.

Heller, Francis H., ed. <u>The Korean War: A 25-Year Perspective</u>. Lawrence, Kansas: The Regents Press of Kansas, 1977.

Herbert, Jerry S., ed. <u>America, Christian or Secular?: Readings in American Christian History and Civil Religion</u>. Portland, Ore.: Multnomah Press, 1984.

Hunt, J.G. and J.D. Blair, ed. <u>Leadership on the Future Battlefield</u>. Washington: Pergamon, 1985.

Ingraham, Larry H., LTC. "Caring is Not Enough: An Uninvited Talk to Army Leaders." <u>Military Review</u>, Vol LVVII (12) Dec. 1987: 45-48.

Johnson, William J. <u>George Washington, the Christian</u>. Nashville, Tenn.: 1919.

Jones, J. William, D.D. <u>Christ in the Camp; or, Religion in Lee's Army</u>. Harrisonburg, virginia: Sprinkle Publications. 1986.

Keegan, John. <u>The Face of Battle</u>. New York: Penguin Books, 1978.

Keegan, John, and Richard Holmes. <u>Soldiers: A History of Men in Battle</u>. New York: Elisabeth Sipton Books-Viking, 1986.

Kushner, Harold S. <u>When Bad Things Happen to Good People</u>. New York: Avon Press, 1983.

LaHaye, Tim. <u>Faith of Our Founding Fathers</u>. Brentwood, Tenn.: 1987. A survey of the religious convictions of the framers of the constitution.

MacArthur, Douglas, GA. "Address to the members of the Association of Graduates, USMA, upon acceptance of the Sylvanus Thayer Award, United States Military Academy, West Point, New York, 12 May 1962.

Marlowe, David H., Ph.D. "Cohesion, Anticipated Breakdown, and Endurance in Battle: Considerations for Severe and High Intensity Combat." Washington: Department of Military Psychiatry, Walter Reed Army Institute of Research. n.d.

Marlowe, David H., Ph.D. "Human Endurance on the Nuclear Battlefield: Thoughts on Prediction and Prophecy." Washington: Department of Military Psychiatry, Walter Reed Army Institute of Research, Washington, D.C., Sept. 1987.

Marshall, Peter, and David Manuel. <u>The Light and the Glory</u>. Old Tappan, N.J.: University Press, 1977. A work arguing that the hand of God may have directed events leading to the creation of America.

Marshall, S.L.A. Men Against Fire. Gloucester, Mass.; Peter Smith, 1978.

Matthews, Richard K. The Radical Politics of Thomas Jefferson. Lawrence, Kan.: University Press of Kansas, 1984.

Morey, Robert A. When Is It Right to Fight? Minneapolis, Minn.: Bethany House, 1985.

Morris, Lynne, ed. The Christian Vision: Man in Society. Hillsdale, Mich.: Hillsdale College Press, 1984.

Noll, Mark. "The Image of the United States as a Biblical Nation, 1776-1865." In The Bible in America: Essays in Cultural History. New York: Oxford University Press, 1982.

Noll, Mark. Christians in the American Revolution. New York: Oxford University Press, 1977.

Nouwen, Henri. Reaching Out: The Three Movements of the Spriitual Life. Garden City, New York: Doubleday, 1966.

Paret, Peter. Clausewitz and the State. New York: Oxford Press, 1976.

Offill, Paul Miller. Stonewall Jackson: A Case Study in Religious Motivation and Its effect on Confederate Leadership and Morale. Univ of Pittsburgh: M.S. Thesis, 1961.

Peterson, Merrill D. Thomas Jefferson and the New Nation. London: Oxford University Press, 1970.

Richards, Warren J. God Blessed Our Arms with Victory. The Religious Life of Stonewall Jackson. New York: Vantage Press, 1986.

Richardson, F.M., MG. Fighting Spirit: A Study of Psychological factors in War. New York: Crane, Russak & Company, 1978.

Roberts, Rovert C. Spirituality and Human Emotion. Grand Rapids, Mich.: Eerdmans Publishing Co, 1982.

Sanders, J. Oswald. Spiritual Leadership. Chicago: Moody Press, 1986.

Schumacher, John. "The Spiritual Dimension of Leadership." An address given at the Baccalaureate Service at the Sergeants Major Academy. 1 July 1991.

Singer, C. Greg. _A Theological Interpretation of American History_. Nutley, N.J.: 1969. The role of theology, and specifically scripture, in shaping the American political and cultural tradition.

Stouffer, Samuel A., et al. _The American Soldier: Combat and its Aftermath_. Vol 2: _Studies in Social Psychology in world War II_. Princeton: Princeton University Press, 1949

Thompson, Parker C. _The United States Army Chaplaincy--From Its European Antecedents to 1791_. Vol I: _History of the United States Chaplaincy_. Washington, 1978.

Tindall, George Brown. _America: A Narrative History_. New York: Cambridge University Press, 1984.

Tuck, Richard. _Natural Rights Theories: Their Origin and Development_. Cambridge, England: Cambridge University Press, 1979.

U.S. Army Chaplain Center and School. _The Unit Ministry Team Concept for the Support of Battle Fatigue Casualties_. Fort Monmouth, New Jersey: 24-25 July 1985.

U.S. Department of the Army. _Army Regulation 165-20: Duties of Chaplains and Responsibilities of Commanders_. Washington, D.C.: 10 May 1985.

U.S. Department of the Army. _Department of the Army Pamphlet 600-63-12: Fit to Win - Spiritual Fitness_. Washington, D.C.: September 1987.

U.S. Department of the Army. _Field Manual 22-103: Leadership and Command and Senior Levels_. Washington, D.C.: June 1987.

U.S. Department of the Army. _Field Circular 16-50: Unit Ministry Team_. Washington, D.C.: September 1986.

Veninga, Robert L. _A Gift of Hope: How We Survive Our Tragedies_. Boston/Toronto: Little, Brown and Co., 1985.

Wakin, Malham M., COL, ed. _War, Morality, and the Military Profession_. Boulder and London: Westview Press, 1986.

White, Morton. _The Philosophy of the American Revolution_. Oxford: Oxford University Press, 1978.

Williams, Cindy Cook. "The Mental Foxhole: The Vietnam Veteran's Search for Meaning." _American Journal of Orthopsychiatry_. Vol 53 (1), January 1983, 4-17.

Woodbridge, John, Mark Noll, Nathan Hatch. _The Gospel in America_. Grand Rapids: zondervan, 1979.

Yolton, John W. _Locke: An Introduction_. Oxford:Blackwell, 1985.

Yolton, John W. _Locke: An Introduction_. Oxford:Blackwell, 1985.